ERNST KRENEK

T004Ø942

TRIO
for Violin, Clarinet, and Piano

AMP 8138

ISBN 978-0-7935-9278-4

Associated Music Publishers, Inc.

DISTRIBUTED BY

HAL•LEONARD®
CORPORATION

7777 W. BLUEMOUND RD. P.O. BOX 13819 MILWAUKEE, WI 53213

TRIO
for Violin, Clarinet, and Piano

I

Ernst Krenek
(1946)

Copyright © 1955 (renewed) by Associated Music Publishers, Inc. (BMI), New York, NY
International Copyright Secured. All Rights Reserved.
Warning: Unauthorized reproduction of this publication is
prohibited by Federal law and subject to criminal prosecution.

II

* Optional

TRIO
for Violin, Clarinet, and Piano

Violin

I

Ernst Krenek
(1946)

Copyright © 1955 (renewed) by Associated Music Publishers, Inc. (BMI), New York, NY
International Copyright Secured. All Rights Reserved.
Warning: Unauthorized reproduction of this publication is
prohibited by Federal law and subject to criminal prosecution.

Violin

II

* Optional

TRIO
for Violin, Clarinet, and Piano

Clarinet in B♭

I

Ernst Krenek
(1946)

Copyright © 1955 (renewed) by Associated Music Publishers, Inc. (BMI), New York, NY
International Copyright Secured. All Rights Reserved.
Warning: Unauthorized reproduction of this publication is
prohibited by Federal law and subject to criminal prosecution.

II

Palo Alto, Calif., June 28, 1946